# NAIL
# DECORATING

# NAIL DECORATING

**Bettina Grabis**

**MUD PUDDLE BOOKS, INC.**
New York, New York

**Photographs by
Paul Maassen**

Text and Concept: Bettina Grabis
Photographs: Paul Maassen
Illustrations: Andrea Leupers
Original Layout: Friederike Pondelik
and Hans-Joachim Schauss
Cover Design: Juergen Pankarz
The fingernails were painted by: Andrea Leupers, Anja von
Gerven, Annette Kleindienst
Thanks to the models: Jana, Nadine, Katja, Lena, Anne Claire,
Amanda, Anna, Kerstin, Tina, Nina & Lisa, Carla, Maria, Kai &
Svenja, Daniela

Published by
Mud Puddle
Books, Inc.

54 West 21st Street, Suite 601,
New York, NY 10010

info@mudpuddlebooks.com

First published in Germany
by moses. Verlag GmbH,
Kempen 1992
Text and illustrations
copyright © moses. Verlag GmbH,
Kempen, 1992.

ISBN: 1-59412-033-1
English translation copyright © 2004
by Mud Puddle Books, Inc.

Printed in China.

10 9 8 7 6 5 4 3 2 1

# Fingernail Painting Secrets:

**We suggest that you use nail polish that is nontoxic, water soluble and peelable (such as the nail polish provided in this kit).**

2. Place the brush in the middle of your nail, almost touching the cuticle. Then, move the brush straight up from the bottom of the nail to the top (the direction is away from your body).

5. Any nail polish that has spilled over the lip may be cleaned with a cotton ball or tissue. If you don't clean the outside of the rim, the dried nail polish residue may act like glue and make it difficult to open the bottle in the future or hardened pieces on the outside of the bottle will fall in making the polish difficult to use.

1. Dip the brush in the nail polish. When you pull it out, lightly wipe it off on the inside lip of the bottle. By doing this you won't apply too much polish nor will your brush drip.

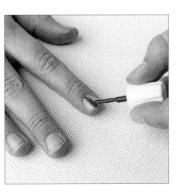

3. Repeat this technique on the left and right side of the nail. Then, let the nail polish dry.

4. Close the bottle as soon as you are finished painting your nails. This prevents the nail polish from drying out.

# Working with Nail Polish

1. We recommend that you paint your nails on a piece of newspaper or towel in case of spills.

2. Shake the bottle thoroughly before you use it.

3. After applying, wait until the nail polish has completely dried. When the nail polish has completed dried, it is easy to apply the next color either over it or next to it. Also, if you change your mind about a design, you can easily remove a new color without destroying the other layer.

4. Be careful not to apply the nail polish too thickly. The thicker the layer, the longer it takes to dry.

5. Spills can easily be removed using a damp cotton ball.

6. Nail polish dries out quickly. Therefore, it is important to close the bottle tight right after use.

# Mixing Your Own Colors

By mixing colors you can produce many different shades. When you mix colors, you can experiment to get the sheen you desire by adjusting the amount of each color you are mixing.

To brighten colors mix them with white polish. To darken colors mix with black.

It is easiest to mix the nail polish on a little plate or plastic tray. Add a few drops of each color onto the plate and stir with a toothpick.

When mixing, make sure that no color gets transferred from one bottle to another bottle. Always remember to wash and dry the brush before dipping it into another nail polish color.

If the nail polish appears to be too thick you can add a little water to dilute it. Do this, however, cautiously. For best results, add water one drop at a time. After each drop of water, shake the bottle thoroughly before determining whether or not another drop is needed.

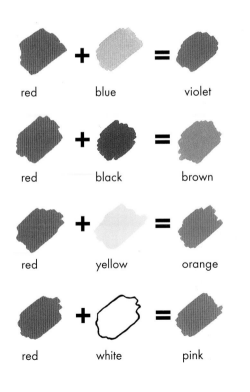

red + blue = violet

red + black = brown

red + yellow = orange

red + white = pink

# Small tools and extras

## Toothpicks

The easiest way to decorate your nails with small dots, fine lines or thin waves is by using toothpicks. Toothpicks help you apply subtle patterns to your nails. Insert the toothpick into a bottle of nail polish, wipe off the excess polish on the lid and, using the tip of the toothpick, draw the desired pattern on your nail.

## A set of brushes

For more precise patterns you'll need different sized brushes. Brushes can be purchased wherever art supplies are sold. Remember, if you only have thick brushes and you needed a finer touch, you can always make a brush thinner by cutting off the bristles to the desired thickness (or, in this case, thinness).

## Gemstones

You can also decorate your painted nails with fake little Gemstones. To do so, apply a tiny drop of nail glue to the stone and attach it with the help of tweezers to your dried fingernail.

## Little stickers

Want to decorate your fingernails with tiny little stickers? All you need to do is paint your nails and let them dry. Then, remove a sticker from its protective paper and apply it to your nail.

## Very glamorous

Here's the secret to nails that sparkle. Simply sprinkle glitter on your polished nails before they're completely dry.
**Tip:** lay your hand flat on a piece of paper so that any excess glitter can be collected easily and put back in the container.

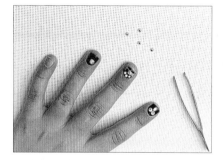

## Be creative

Tiny pearls and bulging eyes are interesting effects. Attach them to your painted and dried nails using nail glue. Tweezers will help you place the little components exactly where you want them.

# Pretty Flowers

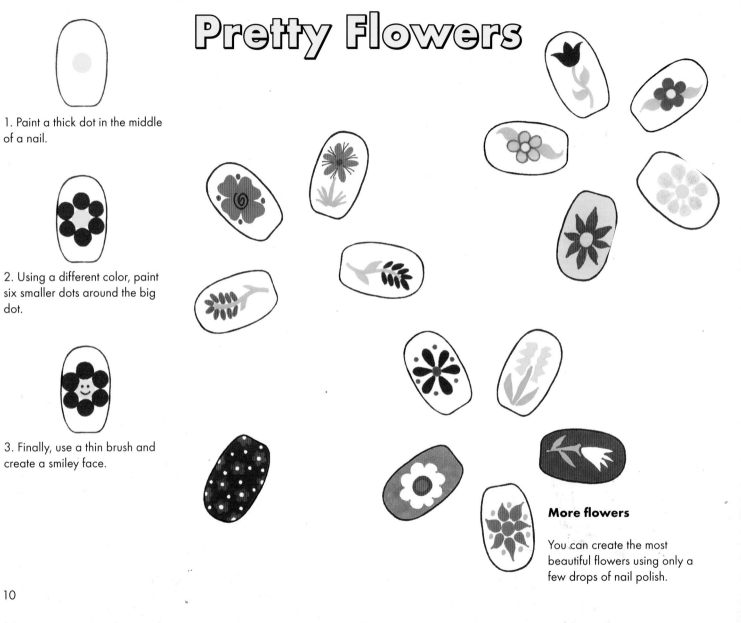

1. Paint a thick dot in the middle of a nail.

2. Using a different color, paint six smaller dots around the big dot.

3. Finally, use a thin brush and create a smiley face.

**More flowers**

You can create the most beautiful flowers using only a few drops of nail polish.

# The Turtle

1. Paint a big light green semicircle in the middle of a nail.

2. With a brush, place dark green specks onto the semicircle.

3. Using a thin brush, add a gray head, tail and legs to the turtle's body.

4. Finally, with the help of a toothpick, draw a black eye and mouth.

# Colorful Butterflies

 1. Paint an arc onto the left side of your nail to create a wing.

 2. Create a second arc on the right side to create a second wing.

 3. Draw a thin black line between the wings for the body. Add two little dots to create a head.

 4. Finish by adding blue dots onto the wings.

# Nail Mail

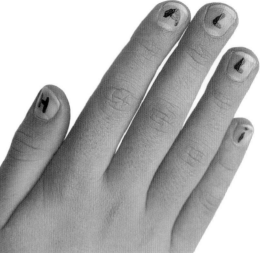

You want to send a friend a quick message? Why not use nail mail?

Simply draw a letter on each fingernail. Use a toothpick so that each letter is clear and easy to read.

Depending on how you will be holding your hands when you "send" your message, you may have to create your letters upside down so that your friend can read them.

14

# Mood Nails

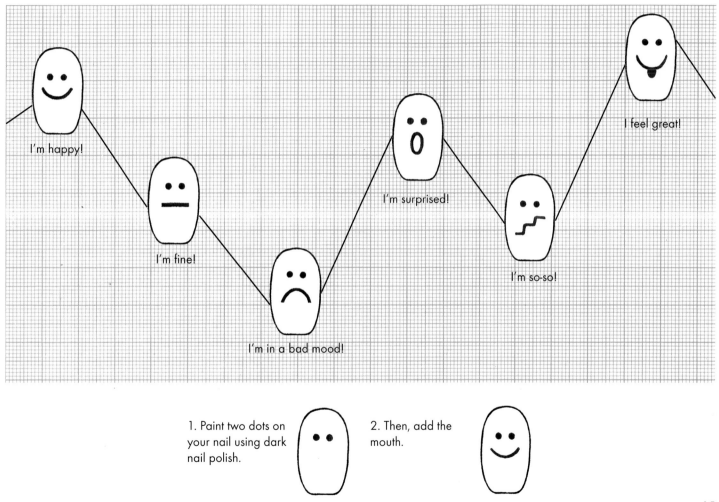

I'm happy!

I'm fine!

I'm in a bad mood!

I'm surprised!

I'm so-so!

I feel great!

1. Paint two dots on your nail using dark nail polish.

2. Then, add the mouth.

# Fruity Nails

1. Paint a small red dot on your fingernail to make a small cherry.

2. Next to the small cherry place a bigger red dot to make a larger cherry.

3. Using a toothpick, draw the black stem.

4. Finally, add a green leave to the stem.

 Pear

 Melon

 Apple

 Strawberry

 Lemon

 Banana

 Grapes

Can you create other fruits to decorate your fingernails?

# Sunset

1. Paint the sun close to the upper edge of your little pinkie.

2. On your ring finger, paint a larger sun lower in the sky. Don't forget the dark sky appearing on the upper edge.

3. On the middle finger, the sun plunges into the water and the dark sky grows larger.

4. On your index finger, you can only see a tiny bit of the sun while the sky slides lower.

5. On your thumb it's completely dark. The whole nail is painted dark blue.

# Beach Nails

Shovel

Bucket

Palm tree

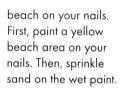

Water ball

At the beach, one thing is certain: it's sandy! With the help of some very fine sand, you can create a realistic looking beach on your nails. First, paint a yellow beach area on your nails. Then, sprinkle sand on the wet paint. As soon as it has completely dried, finish painting your nails by adding a sky and other desired images.

Sun shade

# Be a citizen of the world!

**Create an international look.**

1. Paint a yellow, thick, straight bar on your nail.

2. Next to it, paint a thick red, straight bar.

3. Finally, next to the red, paint a black bar.

Japan

France

Denmark

Cuba

Senegal

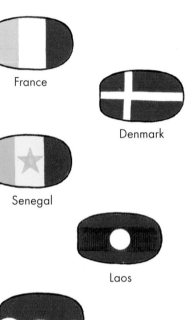
Laos

Spain

Seychelles

Czech Republic

Turkey

# The Nail Clown

1. Paint two thick blue dots on the upper half of your fingernail to create eyes.

2. Dab a thicker red dot below the eyes to create a nose.

3. A thick bent white line below the nose becomes the mouth.

4. Above the eyes add some red hair.

5. Using a toothpick, draw a thin white cross on each eye.

6. Then, add a thin red line on the mouth.

# Potpourri of fun

 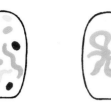   

The clown is not the only image that evokes fun. Party hats, confetti, ticker tape, hard candy, bows and stars in many colors add fun to your nails.

# House of Cards

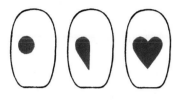  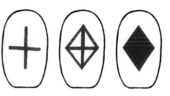 

1. Paint a thick red dot on the upper left side of your nail.

2. Then, drag the dot to the middle of the nail so it looks like a drop.

3. Now, paint a dot on the upper right side of your nail. Drag the paint to the middle of the nail until both halves form the shape of a **heart**.

1. Using black nail polish, paint the **spade** just as you painted the heart—only paint it upside down!

2. The only thing that's missing is the line. Place the brush in the middle of the heart and drag it down.

1. Using red nail polish, paint a red cross in the middle of your fingernail.

2. Connect all corners of the cross.

3. Finally, fill in the total area with red nail polish to complete the **diamond**.

1. Using black nail polish, paint a dot in the upper middle of your nail.

2. Paint two more dots below, one each to the right and left.

3. Finally, place the brush in the middle of the three dots and drag a line down to complete the **club**.

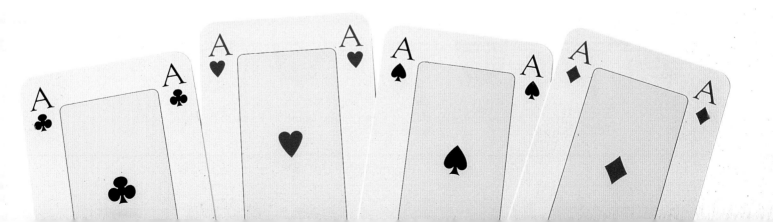

# Peek-a-Boo Nails

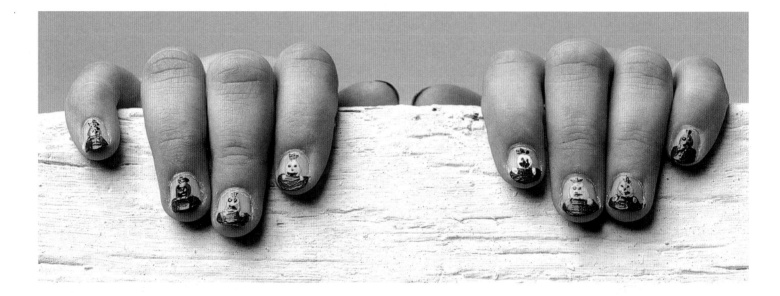

 1. Paint the lower half of your nail blue.

 2. Add a yellow dot to create the head, right above the blue area.

 3. Next to the head, place two little dots to create the hands.

 4. Using a toothpick, draw the face and the hair.

# The Nail Movie

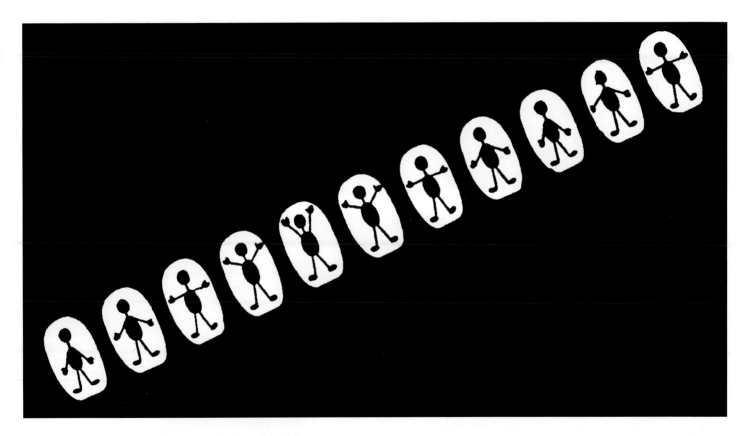

Paint a little stick figure on each one of your nails, changing its position slightly. Soon, you have transformed your fingernails into a mini-movie.

# Black & White

1. Paint one half of your fingernail white.

2. Once the polish is dry, paint the other half of your nail black.

3. Add a black face on the white side of the face.

4. Add a white face on the black side of the face.

# Masked Ball

Fingernails are the perfect shape for unusual masks. Paint a different mask on each nail. Here are some examples:

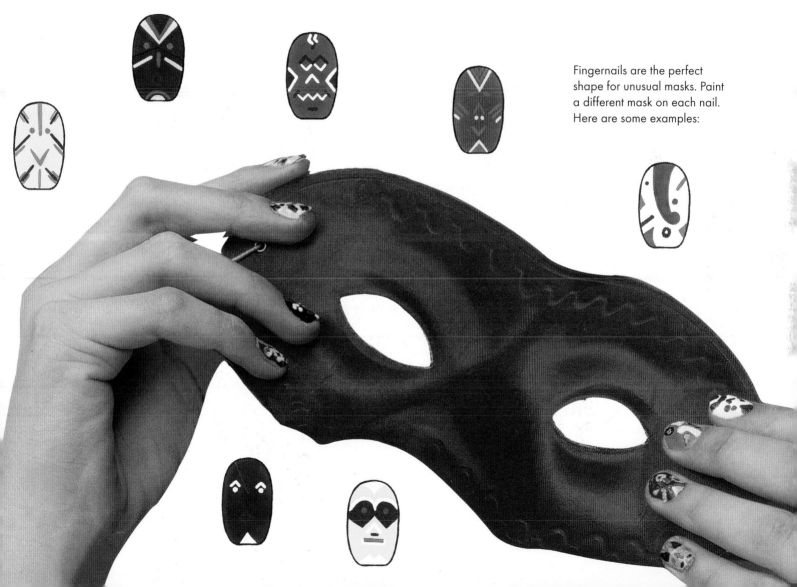

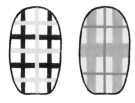

# Scottish plaids and colorful stripes

1. Paint the entire nail red and let the polish dry.

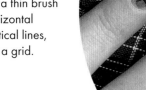

2. With a thin brush add horizontal and vertical lines, forming a grid.

3. Once the polish is dry, draw a second black grid using a toothpick.

**Colorful stripes**

Create a geometrical look with stripes. First, paint your nail in a solid color and let it dry. With a thin brush and a toothpick add different colored stripes.

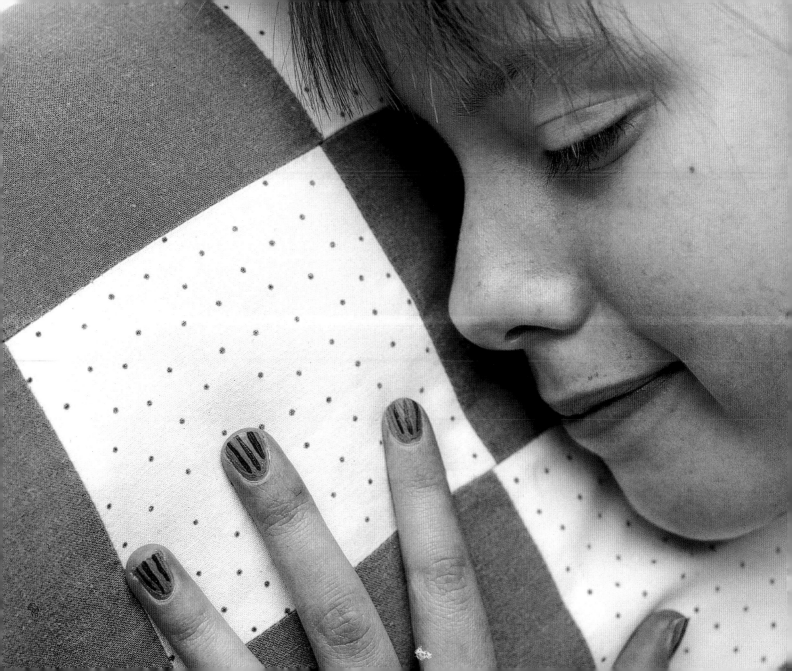

# Multi-colored look of Batik

1. Paint the entire nail in a solid color. Apply the polish thickly.

2. While the base color is still wet, use a thin brush to dab on the next color. Mix the colors slightly.

3. Before the polish is dry, use the same method if you want to add a third or fourth color.

# The Secret of Multi-colored Nails

1. Paint the entire nail blue and let it dry.

2. With a toothpick add red spots on the fingernail and drag the spots across the nail.

3. Quickly add the next color so that they can mix with each other. This creates a great technicolor effect. You can create your own color combinations for endless variety!

# Cats and Dogs

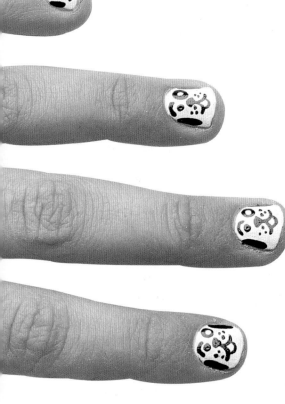

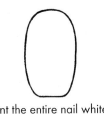

1. Paint the entire nail white and let the polish dry.

2. Paint a black dot in the middle of the nail to create the nose.

3. Using a thin brush add the rest of the dog's or cat's face.

# A Bear to Wear

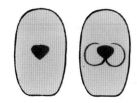

1. Paint a black nose in the middle of the already light brown colored nail.

2. Around the nose draw two half circles.

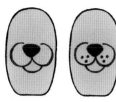

3. Finish the mouth by drawing a curvy line.

4. Add pores around the mouth.

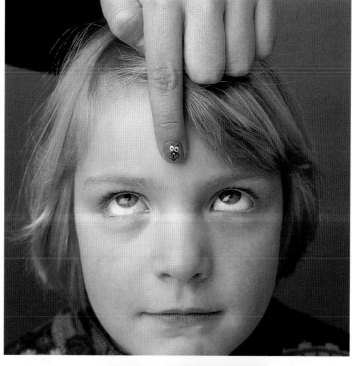

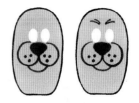

5. Add two white dots to create the eyes above the nose.

6. Paint black eyebrows above the eyes.

7. Once the nail polish is dry, add black pupils.

8. Finish by adding one light brown dab on the nose.

# Swiss Cheese

1. Paint the entire nail yellow and let the polish dry.

2. Add orange colored dots in different sizes.

3. If you add yellow to the dots, they will look like holes.

# ...and Mice (they're nice!)

1. Paint a thick light blue dot in the middle of the nail.

2. Paint little ears at the upper edge of each side of the original dot.

3. As soon as the polish is dry, add tiny pink dots to the ears.

4. For the eyes, paint two white dots in the middle of the head.

5. Once the nail polish is dry, add black pupils to the white dots.

6. Finally, add the black nose at the bottom of the head.

37

# Zebra and Tiger Patterns

1. Paint the entire nail white and let the polish dry.

2. With a thin brush draw thin black stripes. Move the brush slightly to create waves.

3. Leave enough space between the stripes in order to create a realistic zebra-effect.

1. To create a tiger design, first paint the entire nail orange.

2. Once the nail polish is dry, draw irregular black stripes across the nail.

3. The tiger pattern looks best if you leave some space between the stripes.

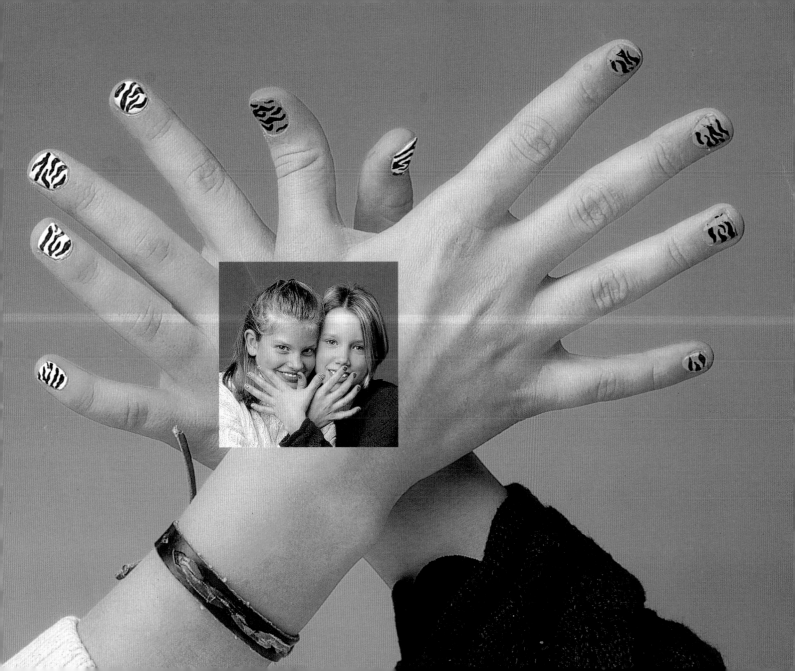

# Dalmatian

1. Paint the entire nail white and let the polish dry.

2. Then, with a thin brush add irregular black dots.

3. Paint the spots in different sizes to create a real Dalmatian look.

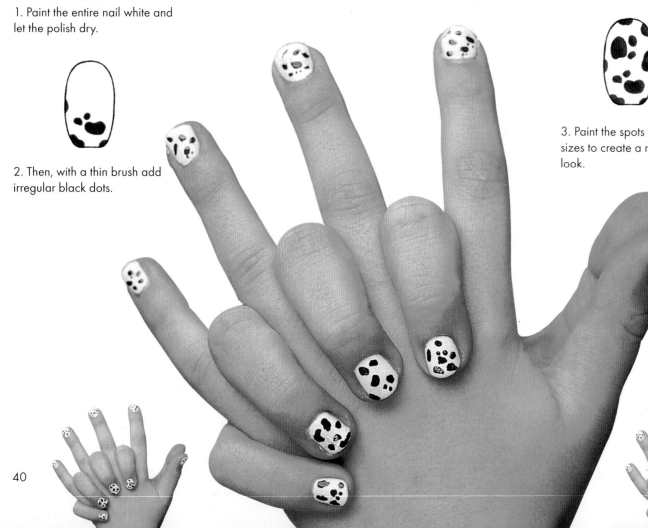

# Leopard

1. First, paint the nail yellow.

2. Once the polish is dray, draw small and irregular loops using a toothpick.

3. This pattern looks especially realistic if you add tiny spots in between the loops.

# Happy Easter

Easter is even more fun if you decorate
your nails with Easter eggs.

 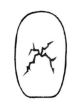 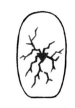  

1. Paint your entire pinkie nail white.

2. Paint the ring finger white and let dry. Then, with a toothpick, add some black broken lines.

3. Repeat step two on your middle finger. However, when dry, add more cracks and a small red beak.

4. Repeat step two on your index finger. When dry, paint larger cracks, an eye and a small yellow area.

5. Repeat step two on your thumb. When dry, add the entire head of the chick.

# Marble

 1: Paint each nail entirely in a solid color.  Apply thickly.

 2. Before dry, add a few drops of white nail polish.

 3. To create a marble pattern, mix the two colors gently with a thin brush.

# Look who's staring out the window!

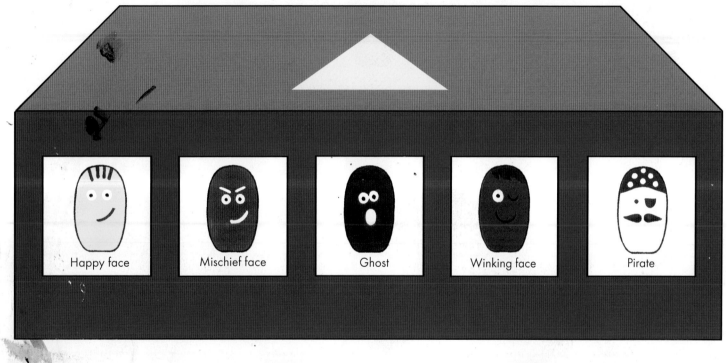

Happy face     Mischief face     Ghost     Winking face     Pirate

1. Paint a nail in your favorite color and let dry.

 2. Using nail glue, glue two tiny bulging eyes in the middle of your nail.

 3. Then, add hair, eyebrows and mouth as desired.

# Fire and Flames

1. Paint an entire nail black and let the nail polish dry.

2. Create red flames by moving a thin brush from the bottom up.

3. Once the red polish has almost dried, add wavy yellow lines.

It's Halloween.

# Fright Night!

Match your nails and outfit.

Blood drop

Witches' Moon

Bat

Pumpkin

Fiery devil

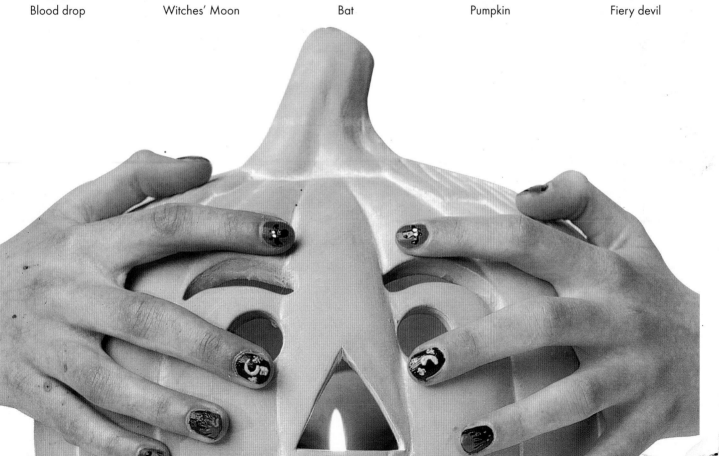

# Happy snail, what's that?

**It's your home and not your hat.**

1. With a toothpick, draw a black coil, starting in the middle of the nail.

2. When dry, fill in the space with red nail polish. Allow to dry.

3. Paint a big yellow snail right below the shell. Allow to dry.

4. Using red nail polish place two little tentacles on the head.

5. Add two tiny dots and a line to create the face.

6. Finally, draw a little grass right below the snail.

# More Squiggles

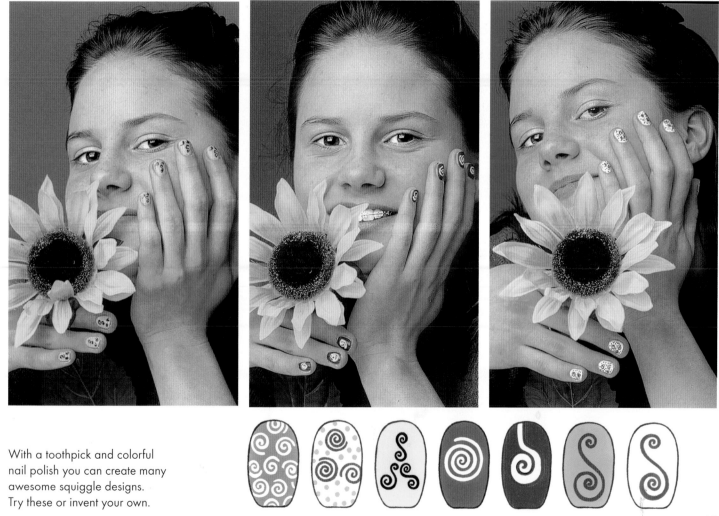

With a toothpick and colorful nail polish you can create many awesome squiggle designs. Try these or invent your own.

# Musical Nails

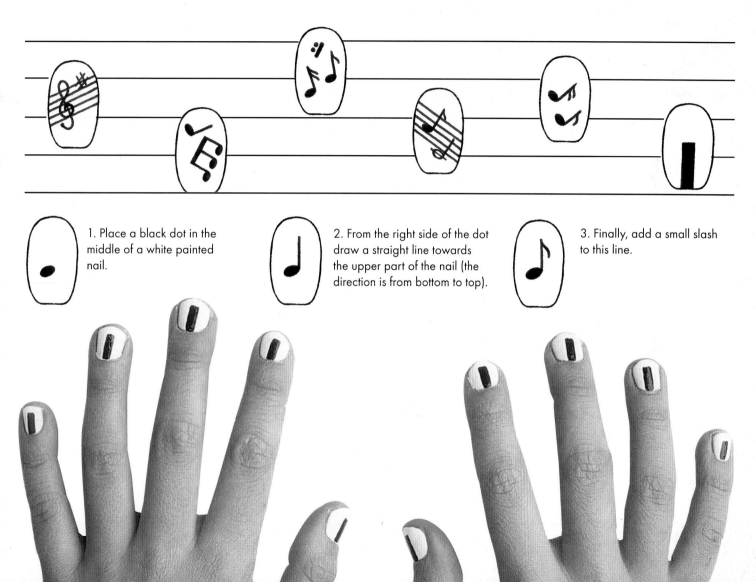

1. Place a black dot in the middle of a white painted nail.

2. From the right side of the dot draw a straight line towards the upper part of the nail (the direction is from bottom to top).

3. Finally, add a small slash to this line.

# Counting Sheep

1. Paint the entire nail blue. Allow to dry.

2. Paint a thick white cloud in the middle of the fingernail.

3. For the tail add a small drop at the edge of the cloud.

4. With black nail polish draw the head and the ear.

5. Draw four lines—the legs—and add a tiny white dot as the eye.

Also, you can beautifully decorate your nails
by painting clouds, stars or a moon.

# Panoramic Nails

  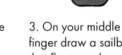  

1. Except for the thumb paint all your nails light blue and let the polish completely dry.

2. Then, paint dark blue waves on every nail, except for your thumb.

3. On your middle finger draw a sailboat that floats on the waves.

4. Now, add clouds, birds and the sun.

5. The theme of the thumb is "under the sea." For this paint a fish on the dark-blue colored nail.

# The Kite

Even toenails can be decorated with many great designs. How about a colorful kite whose tail stretches across all toenails?

In order to easily reach and access your toenails put small cotton balls between your toes.

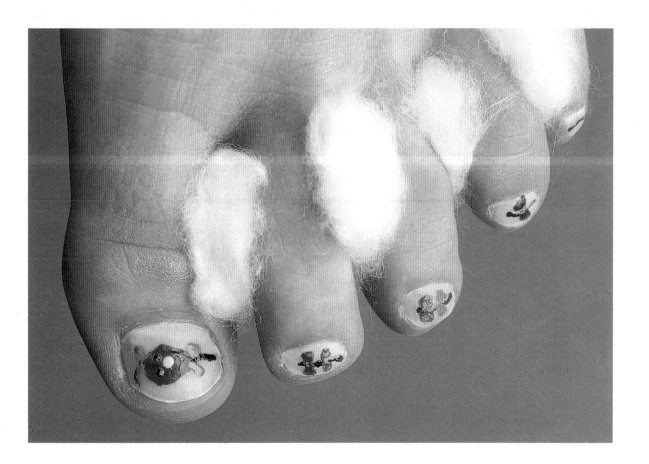

# Color Splotches and Games

1. Paint an entire nail in a solid color and let the polish completely dry.

2. With a brush place a different colored splotch on the nail.

3. Afterwards, add a few small spots around the splotch.

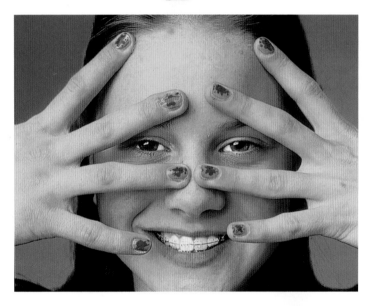

 1. Paint one corner of the nail blue.

 2. Immediately, paint the next corner red and let the two colors run together where they touch.

 3. In an instant, fill in the blank corner with a third color.

# Smurfy Nails

1. Paint the entire nail light blue and let the polish dry.

2. For the cap, paint a thick white bar across the upper part of the nail.

3. With a toothpick outline a black nose and eyes in the middle of the nail.

4. Outline the mouth right below the nose.

5. Fill in the eyes with white nail polish. Place a drop of blue color on the nose and a small red one on the mouth.

6. Finally, all that's missing are the pupils. For this add two tiny dots in the middle of the eyes.

# More funny ideas

Are you getting good at painting your nails? Then, there are many more colorful and amusing ways to decorate your nails using nail polish, a brush and a toothpick.

# Merry Christmas

1. Paint the entire nail light yellow and let the polish dry.

2. For the hat, paint a thick red bar across the upper part of the nail. Also, paint a red bar to the right side of it. Allow to dry.

3. Add a white brim and place a white dot at the tip of the hat. Allow to dry.

4. Below the brim, draw two tiny white lines for the eyebrows. For the eyes, add two small white dots. Once those are dry, add the black pupils.

5. A little below the eyes, paint a white beard. Remember to leave enough space between the eyes and the beard for the nose.

6. Once the beard is dry, add a thick red dot, the nose, and draw a small red line for the mouth.

# More Festivities

There are many more festive motifs with which you can decorate your nails.
Glued-on gemstones and gold and silver stars add extra festive glamour.

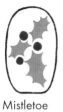

Mistletoe

Starlight

Christmas tree

Hat

Candy cane

Gingerbread

61

# Magic Moments

1. Paint the entire nail blue and let the polish dry.

2. Draw a small yellow star with a toothpick.

3. Add two more stars of the same size.

4. Behind every star, draw a thin trail.

Constellation "Big Dipper"

Starry sky    Chain of stars

Red Mars    Row of stars

**MUD PUDDLE BOOKS, INC.**
New York, New York